# HUSH

Written by Docia Smith

*Illustrated by Derrick Lee Mitchell*

**ASTA PUBLICATIONS**

Copyright © May 2012 by Docia Smith

Library of Congress Cataloging-in Publication Data
    Smith, Docia "Hush"/ Docia Smith

Includes references and index

ISBN: 13: 978-1-934947-61-6
LCCN: 2012935933

First Printing, Asta Publications, LLC, trade paperback edition, May 2012

1. Child Abuse-Non-Fiction. 2. Sexual Abuse-Non-Fiction 3. Self-Help-Non-Fiction. 4. Resource-Non-Fiction I. Title

Illustrations by Derrick Lee Mitchell

For information regarding permission, write to:

Asta Publications, Permissions
P.O. Box 1735
Stockbridge, GA 30281

Printed in the United States of America.

# HUSH

Written by Docia Smith
Illustrated by Derrick Lee Mitchell

When faced with the untimely murder of her own 18 month old grandson Ms. Smith prayed for peace in her spirit and the ideas of the "Comfort Series" books was born. The goal of the series is to make it easier to open the line of communication so the healing process can begin.

The Comfort Series books deal with subjects that parents are often faced with but aren't sure how to open dialogue with their children about issues such as:

Death of a Child (sibling)
Death of a Parent or Grandparent
Incest
Sibling Rivalry
Schizophrenia
Autism
Relationships
and more to come!

For more information or to schedule Ms. Smith for a speaking engagement, visit: www.dociasmith.com.

# Hush little one...

Hush little one you know me.

Hush little one come play with me.

Hush little one your mommy knows I am here.

Hush little one take my hand.

Hush little one follow me up the stairs.

Hush little one, no need for tears.

Hush little one, close your eyes. It won't hurt. I don't want you to cry.

Hush little one it is over now, don't you tell or I'll just lie.

Hush little one I am your friend, for this is our secret to keep between me and you.

Hush little one so that we can do this again.

# Discussion Questions

1. What is molestation and or sexual abuse?

2. What is stranger danger?

3. What is a secret?

4. Are secrets made to be broken?

5. Are there good and bad secrets?

6. Does someone you know make you feel uncomfortable or scared?

# Message for Parents

National statistics show that children all over the world are being sexually abused and/or molestated by someone they know and trust. These numbers are growing everyday, minute by minute.

We are our children's advocate, voice, and protectors from harm. Parents know that you are not alone in this.

There are many resources that are available to you such as the Internet, books, articles, and support groups for you and your child and/or children. When something as horrific as sexual abuse or molestation happens to a child it happens to us all.

# References

1. http://medical-dictionary.thefreedictionary.com/molestation
2. http://encylopedia.thefreedictionary.com/molestation
3. National Hotline Number: 211

# To God Be The Glory

"Hush" was inspired by true events that happened to someone close to me. My hope is to get parents talking with their child and/or children about adults who are making sexual advances toward them. Strangers are not the only people you should be discussing with your children. Many times more often than not it is the people closer to you or maybe living in your home. I ask that you not put a face with danger, because danger looks like you and me. Many times you have invited them into your home and they are feeling safe and warm at your invitation.